© Guinea Pig Education 2018

This pack may not under any circumstances be photocopied, without the prior consent of the publisher.

Written by Sally A. Jones

Contains public sector information licensed under the Open Government Licence v3.0 which can be found on the National Archives website and accessed via the following link: www.nationalarchives.gov.uk/doc/open-document-licence

Published by Guinea Pig Education, 2 Cobs Way, New Haw, Surrey, KT15 3AF

www.guineapigeducation.co.uk

We would like to thank all the children, who attend the Guinea Pig Education tuition classes, for writing the fiction and non-fiction texts included in this book and allowing us to use them. Plus, thank you to the children who have trialled them so diligently.

Instructions

Between the ages of 9 and 12, you will have to complete Standardised.Assessment.Tests (Sats). To help you practise for these tests, we have produced a new series of comprehension booklets. The Standards and Testing Agency states that you have **1 hour** to complete the test, answering the questions in the answer booklet. Read one text and answer the questions about that text, before moving onto the next text. There are three texts and three sets of questions.

When you are completing this booklet, you will see that some questions are followed by a short line or box. This shows that you need only write a word or a few words in your answer. If a question, is followed by a few lines, this gives you space to write more words or several sentences. However, if a question if followed by a large box, you will be expected to give a longer or more detailed answer. You will need to explain your opinion. It is best to write in full sentences for these questions. Read the instructions carefully. Some questions only need you to tick, draw lines to, or circle your answer.

As this is a reading test, you must use the information in the text to answer the questions. Numbers at the side of the page indicate the number of marks you can get for each question.

Before your child tackles the test, parents are advised to read the notes on comprehension at the back of this book.

The tests in this booklet are based on the KS2 Reading Assessment sample papers. It is important to try and complete them in an hour, but it is your choice. The more tests you practise the quicker you will get.

Ellie is a Heroine

The snow in the mountains was melting. It had been a very warm winter. "Looks like the river might overflow," warned Uncle Toby. His words drifted on the wind as Ellie shut the door. "I'm just going down to the village, Uncle," she shouted, heading in the direction of her pony Mitizi's field. Nothing would separate Ellie from her beloved pony. They went everywhere together. If she needed to get some provisions for Uncle, she would ride him down the track to the edge of the village and tether him to a post. She would say, "Wait here little one" stroking his mane and in reply, he would nuzzle his soft nose against her.

On this day, Ellie went over to the shed to get Mitzi but he wasn't there. "He must have wandered out of the gate," she thought to herself. She searched the path but he was nowhere to be seen. Then, she crossed the rickety, old bridge; it seemed to be swaying more than usual. She leaned over the side of the bridge; the water in the river was higher and it was flowing swiftly. Ellie froze! Her heart began to race because she saw something struggling in the river. "Hold on my beauty," she gasped "I am coming." In reply came a weak neigh. Ellie slithered down the bank to the water's edge where she found her little pony stuck in the mud...

Ellie screamed, "Kick, kick as hard as you can." She seized his tail, she tugged at it. "Help! Help!" she yelled but there was no one around. The pony struggled to free himself from the mud but he was stuck fast. The gushing, swirling river was rising rapidly. Would he drown? Fear seized her whole body. She was petrified *(terrified, shaking, shivering)*. Tears streamed down her face but she would not let go.

As Ellie struggled to pull her pony out of the murky water, the river continued to rise. Every time she thought her pony was coming out, he slipped back into the swirling water but she was determined to hang on. At that moment there was a horrible creaking sound as the angry water washed away part of the bridge. In one desperate effort, the pony managed to kick himself free from the mud, push his hooves into the firm reeds of the bank and heave his great body out of the raging water. "Oh thank goodness you are safe," she whispered, hugging him and stroking his soft ears. In return, he licked her hand. After this, they hurried along the path to the village dripping wet and covered in mud. Ellie was able to warn everyone she met of the dangerous bridge and when she arrived in the village she contacted the police who closed the road. Ellie was a heroine. She had rescued Mitzi and saved the lives of many others.

Thomas Edison was one of the world's most successful inventors. Without the devices he invented, the world would not have the technology it has today.
Let's read his story:

His childhood

Thomas Edison was born on February 11th 1842, in the village of Milan, Ohio, USA. During his childhood, he developed a problem that made him partially deaf. From the start, he was a serious little boy, who didn't make friends of his own age and was content with his own company. For this reason, he only spent three months at school, because his mother home schooled him after he became known as a dunce, (a word for a stupid boy in the class).

In fact, he had a natural curiosity and was eager to learn. He loved reading and would read history books from an early age. When his family moved to a new town, he vowed to read every book in the public library. At 9 he received a book on physics, but he did not believe the experiments in it until he had tested them himself, in his science laboratory that was in the basement of his home.

His teenage years

Most children are working hard in school today at the age of twelve, but Thomas had a job as a newspaper boy on a long distance steam train. Because he enjoyed chemistry so much, he set up a laboratory in one of the back carriages. Unfortunately, the chemicals blew up, setting fire to the train so that was the end of that job.

After he saved the life of the stationmaster's baby (from being hit by a train), he found a friend who taught him the trade of telegraph operator. He soon became skilful in taking and sending messages. By fifteen years old, he was in charge of a whole office. His enquiring mind made him determined to understand how the telegraph machine worked and he experimented with a battery in his father's cellar until he understood it. Then, he invented a device called a telegraph repeater, which enabled him to handle messages that came through fast. He experimented with sending more than one message at a time.

A genius at work

Thomas's employers considered him to be a dreamy young person and were quite impatient with him, so he drifted from job to job. However, he carried on working hard on his inventions and spent all his wages on books and scientific apparatus. At the age of twenty-one, he invented a stock ticker for offices. For this, and other inventions in the office, he was paid eight thousand pounds. This is worth about three hundred forty five thousand pounds today. This meant he was able to set up a factory in Newark, New Jersey, with three hundred employees, manufacturing electrical apparatus. Here, in an atmosphere of enthusiasm, he made a lot of money. He sold more than fifty inventions, until poor health made him give up his factory. His first patent was granted in 1869, for the invention of an electric vote recorder.

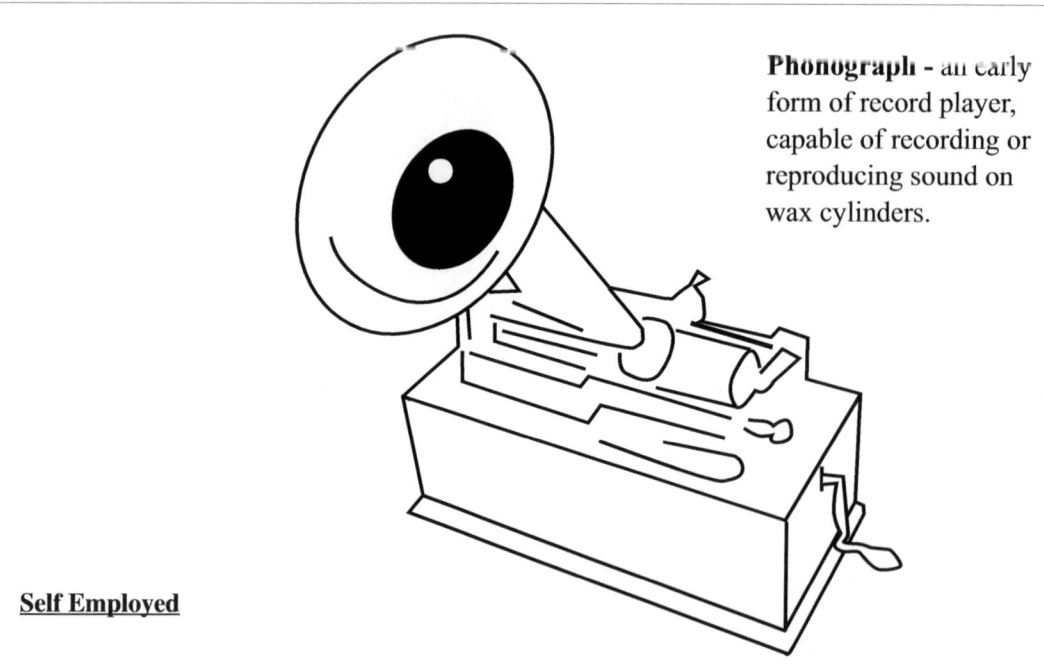

Phonograph - an early form of record player, capable of recording or reproducing sound on wax cylinders.

Self Employed

By now Thomas Edison (in his thirties) had a family and he moved them to a small house with a big laboratory. He thought nothing of working five days and nights without sleep. Most of the time, his wife and children dined alone, for the 'wizard' as he was called, was never to be disturbed. He ate when he was hungry and rested when he was tired, working eighteen to nineteen hours a day. He was as fanatical about his work as some people are about football.

His diligence paid off. He worked on some of his inventions for years, trying to perfect them and spent a lot of money on them, using this motto: 'be sure they are needed or wanted, then go ahead'. In this way, he made more than a thousand inventions: the phonograph (an early form of record player 1878), the long distance telephone, the Edison battery, the carbon microphone used in the telephone and the kinema (a system for making moving motion picture) are a few of the inventions that owe much to Edison. He holds about 1,093 patents for new inventions.

Becoming rich and famous

In 1879, Edison and consulting electrical engineer William Hammer (building on the work of others such as Joseph Swan), invented the electric light bulb. The long lasting, incandescent electric light bulb made him rich, but cost him years and vast expense to perfect. He sent men round the world to get the right filament (you pass an electric current through the filament to make the bulb hot). In 1880, Mento Park was first illuminated, followed by a huge electric station, which lit Orange New Jersey. Edison formed the Edison Electric Light Company in 1878 in New York, with the help of financial backers.

Edison received great honours and many medals for his work. In 1915, he received the Nobel Peace Prize for physics. Wealth and fame did not take away his love of work. It has been said that the secret of his success was due to his ability to spend years of slow, patient experiment on some trivial and uninteresting problem. Edison, a genius of a thousand inventions, had unshakable optimism, a wonderful imagination and these qualities in his character distinguished him from ordinary people. He died in 1931 at the age of eighty-four years. He was famous for the words, 'Genius is one percent inspiration, ninety nine percent perspiration.'

Interesting dolphin facts:

- Dolphins belong to a group of whales called 'toothed whales'. The killer whale comes from this family.

- They are aquatic, warm-blooded mammals that live in the sea or ocean. Dolphins are found all over the world – from the icy seas of the Arctic and Antarctic to the tropical oceans. Some species are even found in the Amazon River.

- A dolphin has a streamlined body, smooth skin, no hair and no ears. Under the dolphin's smooth skin, there is a layer of fat or blubber which helps to keep him warm.

- To swim, they push down with their powerful tail fin and steer with their flippers.

- The colour of their bodies helps camouflage them in the water, so they can't be seen by predators.

- Dolphins can stay under water for a long time. Some dolphins can live underwater for as long as 30 minutes. They have a blowhole on top of their head, so they can come to the surface and breathe.

- Dolphins are social creatures and live in family groups called schools. Often a family will consist of a grandmother, a daughter and her children. They hunt for food together.

- To locate prey, they send out a series of clicks from their throats (echolocation), which bounce off shoals of fish ahead and returns to the dolphin's ear. Fish and squid are their favourite foods.

- They are fast, agile swimmers. They leap out of the water and perform somersaults. Together, they glide across the water to communicate with other dolphins. This is why they enjoy swimming with humans.

- Sometimes a dolphin pushes his head out of the water, looking for food or land.

- Dolphins are very intelligent creatures. In fact, they have an IQ as high as a human toddler!

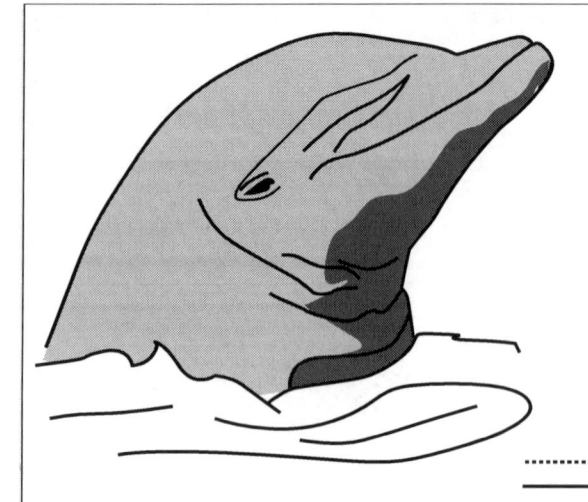

If you're dotty about dolphins, come and experience a <u>dazzling</u> day out at our new <u>*DOLPHIN*</u> CENTRE.

You will learn so much about these delightful creatures. Bring the whole family to the centre, so they can enjoy a day out they'll never forget. Teachers, if you bring your class, they will learn so much. The children will be able to fill in our fun work sheets as they observe the behaviour of these delightful animals up close.

When you come to our centre, you must experience swimming with the dolphins. It would be simply amazing to tell your friends you've been diving deep in the blue water with these gentle creatures. Even if you dare not come in such close contact with our friendly dolphins like Borris or Bethan, you can still watch them perform amazing tricks in the pool, with their trainer, during our daily dolphin show.

Our education centre has a wealth of literature on dolphin behaviour. You can watch some D.V.D clips on how dolphins live in their natural environment or enjoy a showcase of information on endangered wildlife threatened by extinction.

Beside this, there are walks through lovely gardens on your way to the aquarium, which houses hundreds of exotic colourful fish.

When you feel like a break, the Dolphin Café serves freshly made hot drinks in dolphin shaped mugs. It has an amazing selection of pasties and hot meals, with some sensational animal character cakes and biscuits. Definitely worth a try!

Don't forget to call in at our dolphin shop. Take home one of our special ornaments to decorate your home and remind you of your visit.

Where are we?
We are easy to find. Come off the M26 motorway at junction 20 and then follow the signs.

<u>Cost</u>

Adults - £10.00

Children (under 16) £7.50

<u>Opening Times</u>

Summer time – 9am – 6pm

Wintertime – 9am – 4pm

Questions 1-11 are about *The Rescue*

1 Look at the paragraph beginning: *The snow in the mountains...*

Find and **copy** one word meaning carried.

drifted

1 mark

2 *Then, she crossed the **rickety**, old bridge...*

Which word most closely matches the meaning of the word rickety?

Tick **one**

stable ☐

dilapidated ✓

shaky ☐

broken-down ☐

1 mark

3 (a) How can you tell that Ellie sensed danger as she crossed the bridge?

It seemed to been swaying more than usual.

1 mark

(b) What made her heart beat fast?

She saw something struggling in the river.

1 mark

4 Look at the paragraph beginning: *On this day...*

Find and **copy** one word that suggests that the riverbank down to the water's edge was slippery.

Slithered

1 mark

5 *The gushing, swirling river was rising rapidly.*

Give **two** impressions of the river that day

1. fast

2. Intence

2 marks

6 Look at the paragraph beginning: *Ellie screamed...*

How does the writer show that Mitzi, Ellie's pony, was in great danger?

Give **two**.

1. "Would he drown?"

2. "Fear seized her whole body."

2 marks

7 Look at the paragraph beginning: *As Ellie struggled...*

(a) Write down three things you are told about the river.

1. _murky water_
2. _Swirling water_
3. _raging water_

3 marks

(b) What do you think caused this to happen?

The snow was melting in the mountins

1 mark

8 Write down three things you are told about Ellie's horse as he makes a desperate effort to save himself?

1. _He kicked him self free._
2. _Push his hooves in the reeds_
3. _heave his great body out of the water._

3 marks

9 **Find** and **copy** two examples of personification that are used to describe the water.

1. _____
2. _____

1 mark

10 (a) Why is Ellie labelled a heroine at the end of the story?

_____

1 mark

(b) What is a heroine?

_____

_____

1 mark

11 What was revealed at the end of the story?

Tick one

Ellie went straight home. ☐

She saved peoples' lives. ☐

Ellie phones Uncle Toby. ☐

Uncle Toby takes the horse box to Ellie. ☐

1 mark

Questions 12- are about *Thomas Edison*

12 Circle the correct option to complete each sentence below.

(a) Thomas Edison was born on February 11th...

- 1895
- 1927
- 1842
- 2006

1 mark

(b) While he was being taught at home by his mother, the young Thomas loved to...

- do maths
- draw
- read history books
- play the piano

1 mark

(c) At the age of fifteen, Thomas's <u>first</u> invention was...

- a stock ticker
- a telephone
- a device called a telegraph repeater
- an electronic light bulb

1 mark

(d) Thomas carried on working hard on his inventions. At the age of twenty one, he was paid....

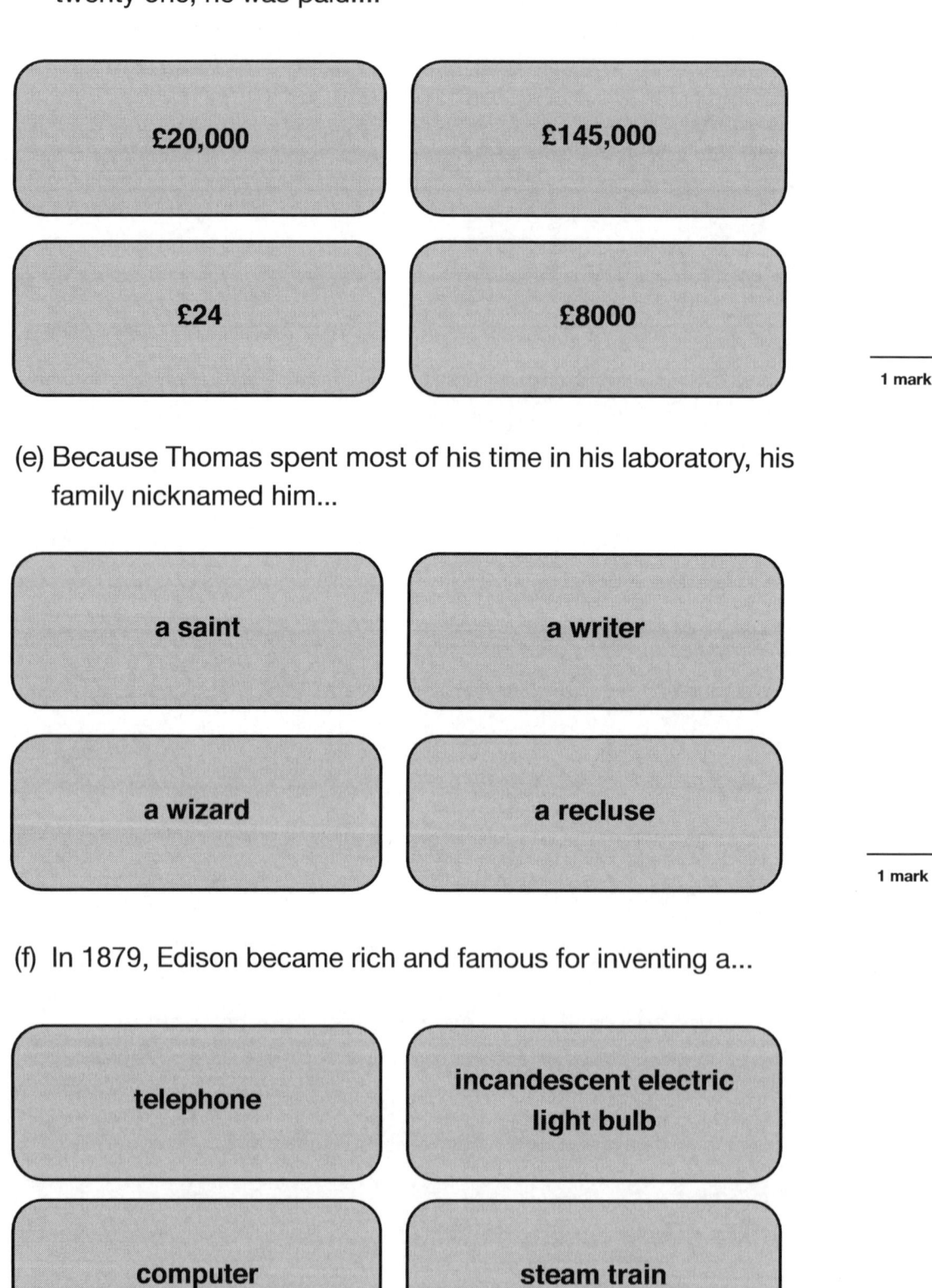

£20,000

£145,000

£24

£8000

1 mark

(e) Because Thomas spent most of his time in his laboratory, his family nicknamed him...

a saint

a writer

a wizard

a recluse

1 mark

(f) In 1879, Edison became rich and famous for inventing a...

telephone

incandescent electric light bulb

computer

steam train

1 mark

13 Look at the paragraph beginning: *Thomas Edison was born on ...*

Find and **copy** one word that shows Thomas Edison was quiet and thoughtful..

_____

1 mark

14 *He became known as a **dunce**...*

Which word most closely matches the meaning of the word dunce?

Tick **one**

genius ☐

clever ☐

fool ☐

naughty ☐

1 mark

15 How can you tell that the young Thomas did not fit in at school?

_____

_____

_____

1 mark

16 Look at the paragraph beginning: *In fact, he had a natural curiosity...*

Find and **copy** two phrases that suggests he was actually eager to learn.

1. _____

2. _____

2 mark

17 *His enquiring mind made him determined to understand how the telegraph machine worked and he experimented with a battery in his father's cellar until he understood it.*

Give **two** impressions of what this suggests about Thomas as an adult and his attitude to his work.

1. _____

2. _____

2 marks

18 Look at the paragraph beginning: *Thomas's employers considered him to be...* to the sentence ending: *...scientific apparatus.*

What impression do you get of Thomas in his early jobs?

Give **two**.

1. _____

2. _____

2 marks

19 Write down three things you are told about Thomas that helped change his life.

1. _____

2. _____

3. _____

3 marks

20 Look at the paragraph beginning: *By now Thomas Edison (in his thirties)...*

Find and **copy** an adjective which shows that work was very important in his life.

_____

1 mark

21 (a) Why did Edison's family call him the 'wizard' do you think?

_____
_____

1 mark

(b) What signs are there that prove Edison was obsessed with his work?

_____
_____
_____

1 mark

22 (a) What evidence is there to show that Thomas wanted to invent useful things that would improve peoples lives'?

_____

_____

1 mark

(b) What evidence is there to show he would go to any length to perfect his inventions?

Give **two** reasons.

1. _____

2. _____

2 marks

23 (a) What does *incandescent* mean?

_____

1 mark

(b) What does *first illuminated* mean?

_____

1 mark

(c) What does *unshakeable optimism* mean?

_____

1 mark

(d) What does *distinguished him* mean?

_____

1 mark

24 Do you think Edison's diligence helped him become rich and famous?

Tick **one**

yes ☐

no ☐

maybe ☐

Explain your choice fully using evidence from the text.

3 marks

25 In what ways might Edison's character appeal to many readers?

Explain fully, referring to the text in your answer.

[answer box]

3 marks

26 Using information from the text, tick one box in each row to show whether each statement is **true** or **false**.

	True	False
He built on the work of Joseph Swan to invent the electric light bulb.		
Edison received a Nobel peace prize.		
He died at the age of 96.		
He died very poor.		

1 mark

Questions 27-37 are about *Dolphins*

27 *A dolphin has a **streamlined** body, smooth skin, no hair and no ears.*

What does the word *streamlined* suggest about the dolphin's body?

_____

_____

_____

1 mark

28 *They are aquatic, warm-blooded mammals that live in the sea...*

Why are dolphins known as aquatic, warm-blooded mammals?

_____

_____

_____

1 mark

29 **Find** and **copy** one word that tells your what the dolphin has that keeps him warm.

_____

1 mark

30 Give two reasons why dolphins are good hunters.

1. _____

2. _____

2 marks

31 *They are fast, **agile** swimmers.*

What does the word *agile* suggest about how dolphins swim?

_____

_____

1 mark

32 Look at the article beginning: *If you're dotty about dolphins, come...*

What does the word *delightful* suggest about dolphins?

_____

_____

_____

1 mark

33 Look at the paragraph beginning: *When you come to out centre...*

Find and **copy** a group of words that show alliteration

_____

1 mark

34 Why do you think D.V.D clips, on how dolphins live in their natural environments, are shown to visitors?

_____

_____

1 mark

35 (a) Give the meaning of the phrase *endangered wildlife threatened by extinction.*

_____

_____

1 mark

(b) What does *exotic* mean?

_____

1 mark

(c) What does *sensational* mean?

_____

1 mark

36 According to both texts, why would it be enjoyable to swim with dolphins?

_____

_____

_____

2 marks

37 What information is provided at the end of the article?

Tick **one**

The entrance fee is £10 for both adults and children. ☐

The Dolphin Centre is closed in the winter. ☐

The centre is located off the M40 motorway at junction 10. ☐

The Dolphin Centre is open from nine o'clock in the morning till six o'clock in the evening, during the summer months. ☐

1 mark

ANSWERS

The answers to these questions have been written and discussed by children who attend Guinea Pig Education tuition classes. Therefore, they are only suggestions and you may be able to give more detailed answers.

Answers

1. drifted

2. dilapidated

3. (a) When she crossed the bridge, it was swaying more than usual. The water level was higher than usual and the river was flowing rapidly, which means very fast. It says "she froze" which suggests she was very frightened and could not move.
   (b) She saw something struggling in the river. The word 'struggling' suggests he was stuck in the mud and because the water was rising, he was in danger of drowning.

4. slithered

5. The river was flowing very rapidly and uncontrollably. There was a large amount of water moving in a twisting, spiralling pattern. The water level was increasing at an extremely fast pace.

6. He builds up suspense and tension using short sentences, repetition and punctuation - exclamation marks. He uses words that show fear like "petrified" and "struggled". He shows the power and force of the water by using words like "gushing" and "swirling." At the end of this paragraph, he leaves the reader wondering what will happen.

7. (a) The river was still rising. The colour of the water was "murky", which means, dirty, muddy, cloudy. The water was "swirling". The 'angry' water washed away part if the bridge. The water was 'raging,' this suggests the river was violent and uncontrollable.

   (b) The river was swelling because the snow in the mountains was melting, because, although still winter, it was getting warmer.

8. The pony managed to kick himself free from the mud. He pushed his hooves into the firm reeds of the bank. He managed to heave his great body our of the raging water.

Answers

9. angry water and raging water

10. (a) Ellie is labelled a heroine because she saved Mitzi and warned everyone she met and the police, who closed the road, that the bridge had broken.

    (b) A heroine is a girl or woman who is admired for he courage or an outstanding achievement. A brave woman, a woman of courage, a hero.

11. She saved peoples' lives.

Answers

12. (a) 1842 (b) read history books (c) a device called a telegraph repeater (d) £8000 (e) a wizard (f) incandescent electric light bulb

13. serious

14. fool

15. He had no friends his own age; he kept his own company; and he was labelled a dunce.

16. He loved reading and would read history books from an early age; he vowed to read every book in the public library; he did not believe the experiments in it until he had tested them for himself.

17. He was inquisitive and determined to investigate how the machines worked; he persevered and experimented until he understood; he was very curious and intent on understanding how things worked; he didn't give up.

18. He was always preoccupied with his own thoughts, so he didn't apply himself to his work and his employers became frustrated with him; his head was full of his own ideas; he didn't appear to listen, focus or concentrate on his work; he didn't do what his employers wanted; he didn't meet the requirements of his early jobs; he moved aimlessly from job to job.

19. He worked hard on his inventions; spent all of his wages on books and scientific apparatus; he was paid £8000 for his early inventions, giving him funds to establish a factory with 300 employees; he sold more than fifty inventions; he obtained his first patent in 1859.

20. fanatical

Answers

21. (a) He locked himself away; his house was small but it had a big laboratory, where he was constantly experimenting and concocting new ideas; he worked 18/19 hours a day, sometimes going for days without sleep, only eating when he was hungry, thereby showing super human strength; he was never to be disturbed. His inventions were unique (unheard of), at that time, so it was like he was concocting spells.

    (b) He worked on his inventions for years trying to perfect them; he went without sleep; he missed family meals and only ate when he was hungry; his family and visitors were not allowed to interrupt him when he was working.

22. (a) his motto was "be sure they are needed or wanted, then go ahead."

    (b) He was willing to focus and experiment for years on a trivial, uninteresting problem until it was perfected; he was willing to invest his own money in his inventions; in order to source the perfect parts for his inventions, he sent men around the world.

23. incandescent - brilliant, luminous, giving off light; illuminated - light up; unshakeable optimism - unchangeable, deep feeling of hopefulness and cheerfulness about the future; distinguished him - set him apart.

24. Child's own ideas. Three well developed reasons. Some ideas are listed below:

    Yes - his hard work and persistence meant that he designed a lot of different inventions. Once he had completed an invention, he did not stop working, but started on a new idea. This meant he had money coming in from lots of different places. It also meant that he earned people's trust. This helped him find financial backers and enabled him to fund further inventions.

    - Edison enjoyed working out trivial problems and his hard work meant that he was successful at his job and meant he was able to pay people to work for him. He also was able to learn from others.

    - Edison's life shows how much effort you need to succeed. Plus, his inventions helped others build more technological devices today e.g. phones, laptops, i-pads.

Answers

No - his diligence was not the reason he became rich and famous. He became rich and famous because the inventions he created were products people needed. His motto was "be sure they are needed or wanted, then go ahead." His inventions were unique and were useful, and as such became products people desired to own.

- He developed the work of others and had other people help him, he was not always working alone. For instance, when he created the electric light bulb, he built on Joseph Swan's work and he consulted electrical engineer William Hammer. Plus, he also sent men round the world to source the perfect materials.

25. He was hardworking, patient and conscientious. Even at the age of nine, he put effort into his work. It says in the text that "he vowed to read every book in the library." This shows us he was an avid learner, willing to persevere and very diligent. He was cheerful and had a wonderful imagination; he was passionate about inventing and he did not let wealth and fame change him; he only invented items that would be of use and would change peoples lives for the better; he thought about the greater good, inventing items which society needed; even when he became a great man, he continued to solve lowly and uninteresting problems; his work achieved public acclaim, he was a celebrity and received the Nobel Peace prize for physics, which is one of the highest accolades you can get; he was a genius; he was an inventor and would have been an interesting person to meet.

26. True, true, false, false

Answers

27. The word streamlined suggests the dolphin's body is perfectly designed, so that it can move easily and speedily through the water. It's body is smooth and sleek. Dolphin's bodies are designed to present very little resistance to the flow of water, which is why they are hairless and have no ears.

28. Dolphins are known as aquatic, warm-blooded mammals because although they live in the water, they are not fish. A character of mammals is to have warm-blood, which means that dolphins have a constant body temperature, which is normally above the environment in which they live.

29. blubber

30. Dolphins are good hunters because the colour of their body makes them invisible in the water. They can stay under the water for a long time. They hunt in a family group. They use echolocation to find their prey. They are fast, agile swimmers.

31. The word agile suggests that dolphins are able to move quickly and easily through the water.

32. The word delightful suggests the dolphins are a source of great pleasure and they will make people feel joyful or happy. It suggests they are charming, entertaining and amusing.

33. diving deep

34. D.V.D clips are shown to visitors to inform or teach them about how dolphins live in their natural environment, so that visitors will learn how important it is to respect and look after planet Earth, so we don't destroy the dolphins' natural home.

35. (a) The phrase endangered wildlife threatened by extinction means wild animals who are seriously at risk of disappearing from our planet, they are in danger of dying out.

Answers

(b) Exotic means something which is originally from a distant foreign country. An item which is exotic is often attractive or striking because it is colourful or out of the ordinary.

(c) Sensational means something which causes great public interest and excitement, something which is shocking or scandalous. Yet, in this context, it is used in an informal way, suggesting that the animal character cakes and biscuits are very good indeed, very impressive , stunning and wonderful.

36. It would be enjoyable to swim with dolphins because they bring so much pleasure and are 'delightful.' They enjoy swimming in family groups and therefore, also love swimming with humans. They are fast agile swimmers and you will be able to see them up close leaping out of the water, performing somersaults and other amazing tricks.. Everyone you know will be jealous and you'll be able to tell them all about how awesome it was, it is an incredible opportunity. The dolphins are very gentle and friendly.

37. The Dolphin Centre is open from nine o'clock in the morning till six o'clock in the evening, during the summer months.

What am I doing when I do comprehension?

I am answering comprehension questions. →	These questions test my reading ability.
I am reading fiction which is a narrative or story. **or**	I am reading non-fiction which is information on a certain topic.

My answers will show how much I understand about the meaning of the text.

I am learning these skills:

I am retrieving or finding answers from a text. →	This means I am identifying key details (or points) in a text.

The questions on my texts often start like this... →	How did... How can you tell... How would you... According to the text, how could you... How far... Where does... What does/did/was... Which of these... Using information from the text, write down three things... Identify key details... Give two reasons why...
I know I can find <u>these</u> answers in the text.	

Other questions tell me to:

Match, circle or tick
the correct answer

---

or

Complete the table, summarise the main events,
find and copy a group of words from the text.

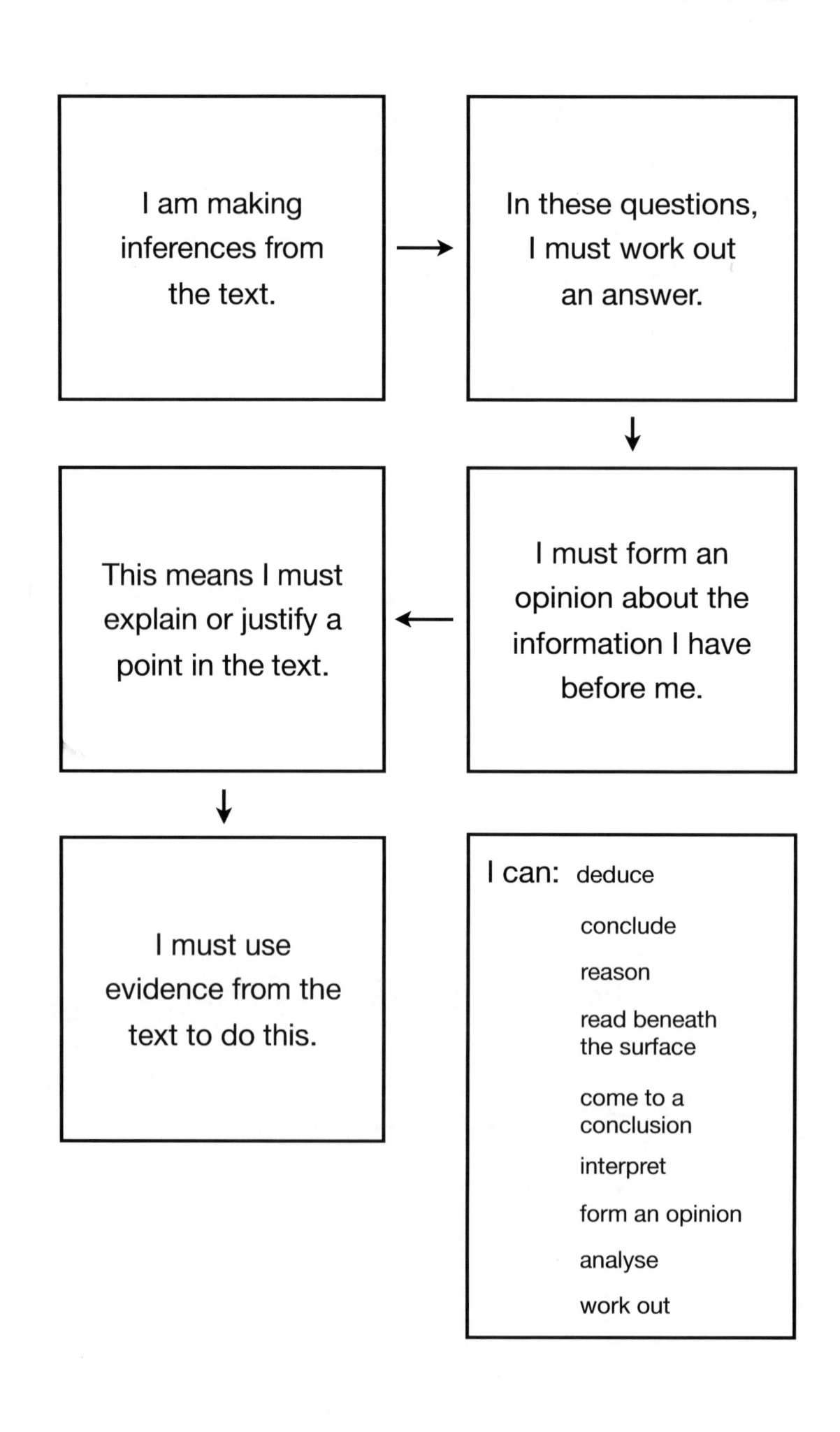

```
┌─────────────────────┐      ┌─────────────────────┐
│                     │      │                     │
│   I am making       │      │  In these questions,│
│   inferences from   │─────▶│  I must work out    │
│   the text.         │      │  an answer.         │
│                     │      │                     │
└─────────────────────┘      └─────────────────────┘
                                        │
                                        ▼
┌─────────────────────┐      ┌─────────────────────┐
│                     │      │  I must form an     │
│  This means I must  │      │  opinion about the  │
│  explain or justify a│◀────│  information I have │
│  point in the text. │      │  before me.         │
│                     │      │                     │
└─────────────────────┘      └─────────────────────┘
           │
           ▼
┌─────────────────────┐      ┌─────────────────────┐
│                     │      │  I can:  deduce     │
│                     │      │                     │
│  I must use         │      │          conclude   │
│  evidence from the  │      │                     │
│  text to do this.   │      │          reason     │
│                     │      │                     │
│                     │      │          read beneath│
│                     │      │          the surface│
│                     │      │                     │
│                     │      │          come to a  │
│                     │      │          conclusion │
│                     │      │                     │
│                     │      │          interpret  │
│                     │      │                     │
│                     │      │          form an opinion│
│                     │      │                     │
│                     │      │          analyse    │
│                     │      │                     │
│                     │      │          work out   │
└─────────────────────┘      └─────────────────────┘
```

The questions often start and continue this way...	Explain how... supports the idea... (a) making appropriate reference to the text (b) or infer from the text
Explain what this suggests... using evidence from the text.	Refer to or recognise these...
How does the first paragraph suggest that... How can you tell...	How do these words make the reader feel... How do we know...

How does the information in paragraph... make him sound.	What impressions do we get?
Summarise... Look at... Compare two...	Why were/was... Why did... In what way might...
Using the information... tick one box to show whether the statement is true or false.	When you use evidence in the text you can refer to it or write it in a quote using "................"

These answers will help you form opinions about characters - how they think and behave - and about the situations they face.

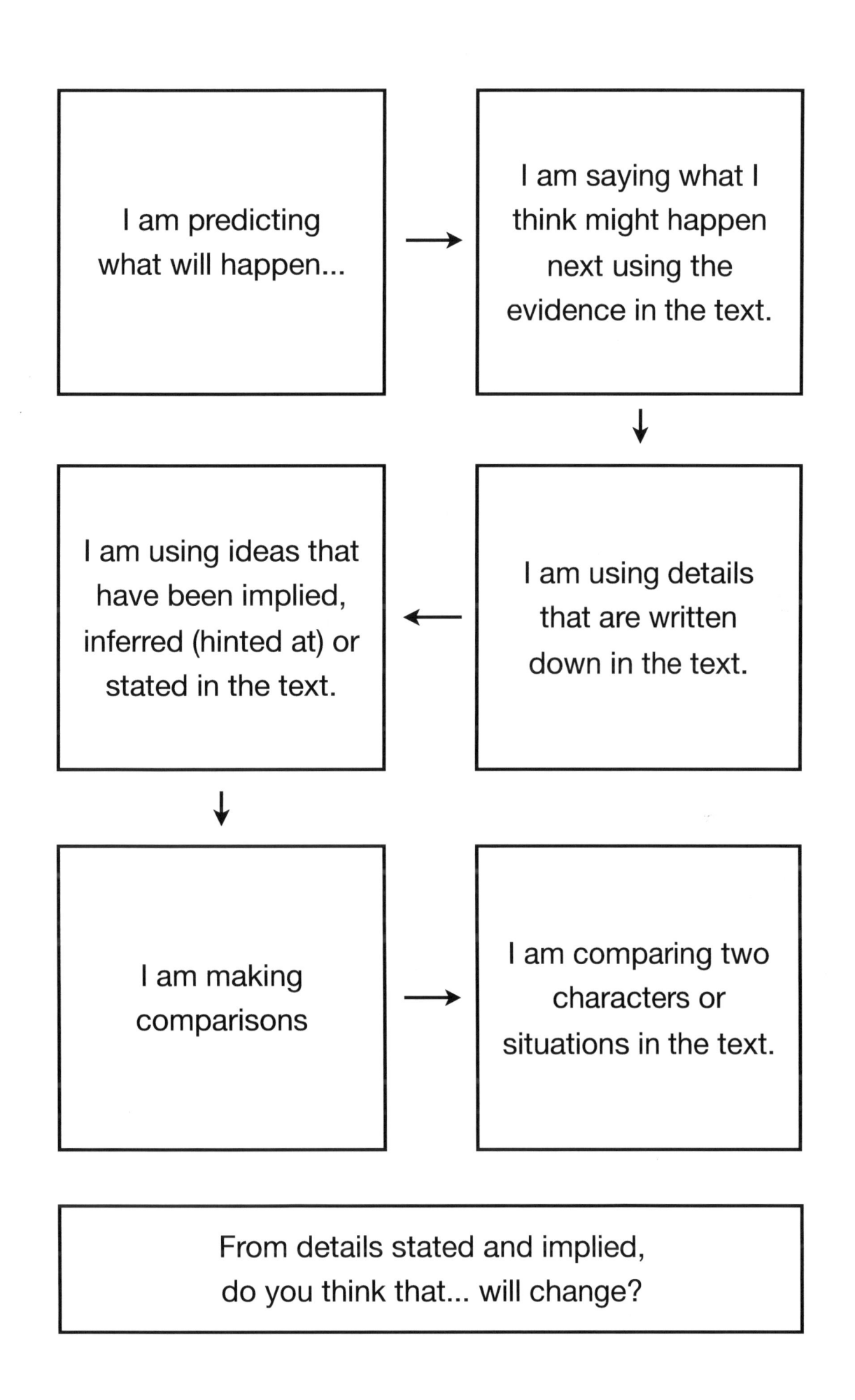

I am predicting what will happen... →	I am saying what I think might happen next using the evidence in the text. ↓
I am using ideas that have been implied, inferred (hinted at) or stated in the text. ↓	← I am using details that are written down in the text.
I am making comparisons →	I am comparing two characters or situations in the text.

From details stated and implied, do you think that... will change?

I am answering questions about language. →	Finding the meanings of particular words and phrases will help my vocabulary.
I know the writer chose particular words and phrases to enhance the meaning **so**	the reader can understand what he or she means.

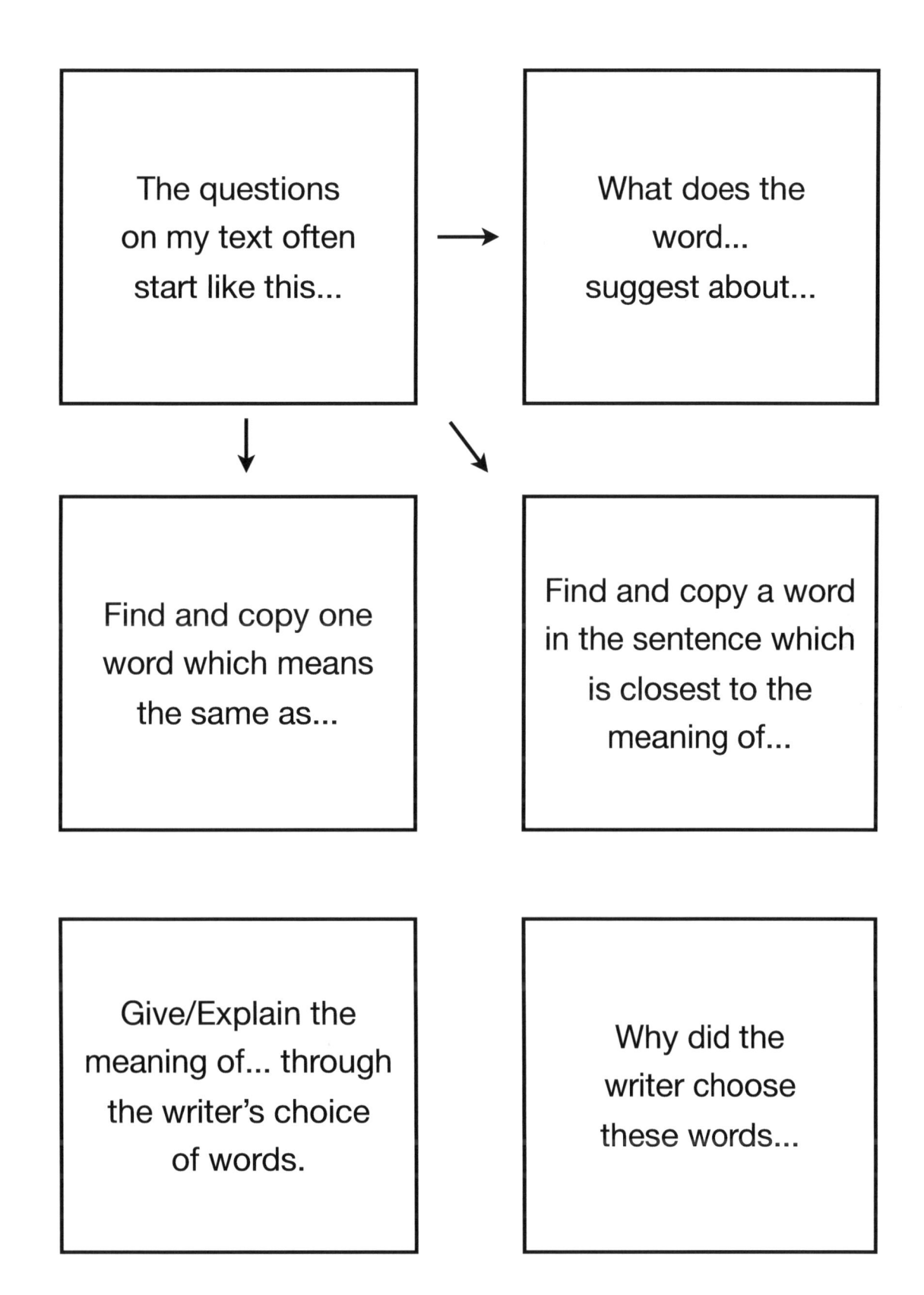

- The questions on my text often start like this...
- What does the word... suggest about...
- Find and copy one word which means the same as...
- Find and copy a word in the sentence which is closest to the meaning of...
- Give/Explain the meaning of... through the writer's choice of words.
- Why did the writer choose these words...

Identify/explain the meaning of these words in the context

Which word closely matches or is closest in meaning to...

Find and copy one word that...

Give an interpretation of...

Give two impressions of...

Explaining words in the context just means what the words mean in a particular text.

Printed in Great Britain
by Amazon